BY MICHAEL PATRICK

Three Rivers Press, New York

Concept and Direction
Mike Dowdall

Written by
Patrick Welch

Editor
Jennifer Woodhead

Technical Illustration
Mark Schlimme

Photography
Jenifer Cady
Tom Probasco
Rush Photography
Troy Staten

Art Director, Production Director and Design
Nina Schreiner

Published by Three Rivers Press, 201 East 50th Street, New York, New York 10022.
Member of the Crown Publishing Group.

Random House, Inc. New York, Toronto, London, Sydney, Auckland
http://www.randomhouse.com/
Three Rivers Press is a trademark of Crown Publishers, Inc.
Printed in Hong Kong
Library of Congress Cataloging-in-Publication Data is available upon request
ISBN 0-609-80110-4

10 9 8 7 6 5 4 3 2 1
First Edition

Desenex
ANTIFUNGAL POWDER
CURES ATHLETE'S FOOT
Relieves Itching & Burning
FRESH SCENT
by MENNEN

Dedicated to

Meagan and Courtney,

who will one day have

babies of their own.

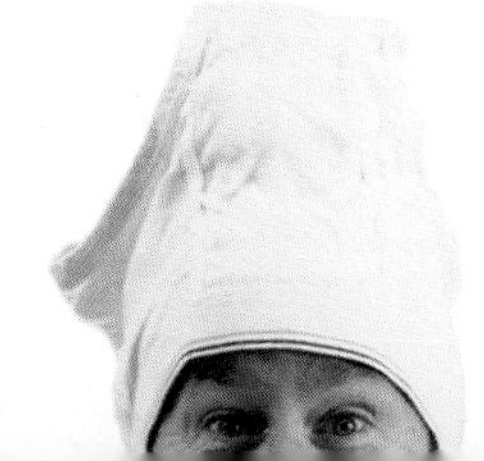

They're messy.

They're whiny. They throw their food.

They're totally dependent, unbelievably selfish, and endlessly demanding. They have to be fed when they're hungry, changed when they're wet, and coddled when they're cranky. We are expected to wake up before them, clean up after them, laugh delightedly at their absurd antics and incomprehensible gurglings, and through it all think of them as miracles of nature and count ourselves lucky to have them. And there is the real miracle:

We do.

Baby likes to be in control.

He recognizes

mportance of a well-rounded diet.

He rarely

misses a chance to commune with nature.

Despite their playful curiosity, they don't seem

now the true functions of certain objects.

He has to be fed when he's hungry. He has to be coddled when he's cranl

e has been known to throw his food. But he doesn't like to be called "Baby."

Baby always enjoys a nice long soak

Somehow you
know he's near

BUT THIS

IS DEFINITELY

NOT THE

PLACE

you're most likely to find him.

This is the legend
Of the Little Misters
Who raise the lid
And surprise their sisters

They come around
In the cold midnight
To lift it up
And hold it tight

They live for the shrieks
Of Auntie and Mum
When icy rim
Meets toasty bum

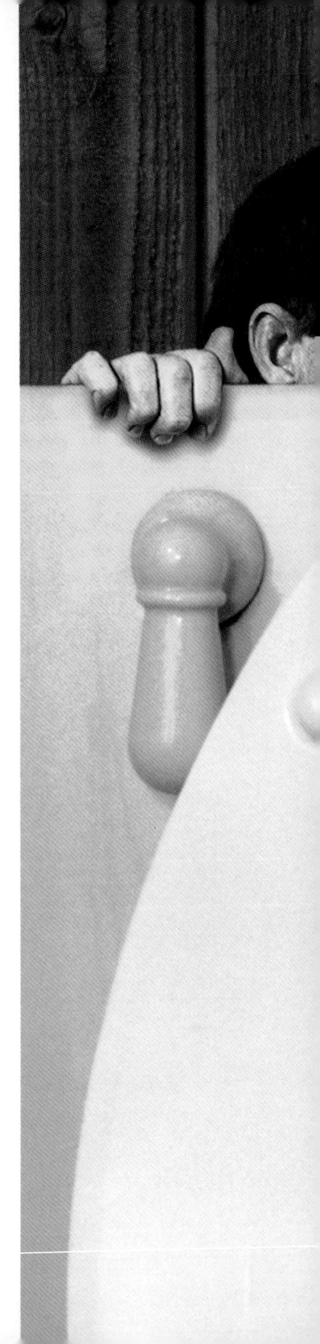

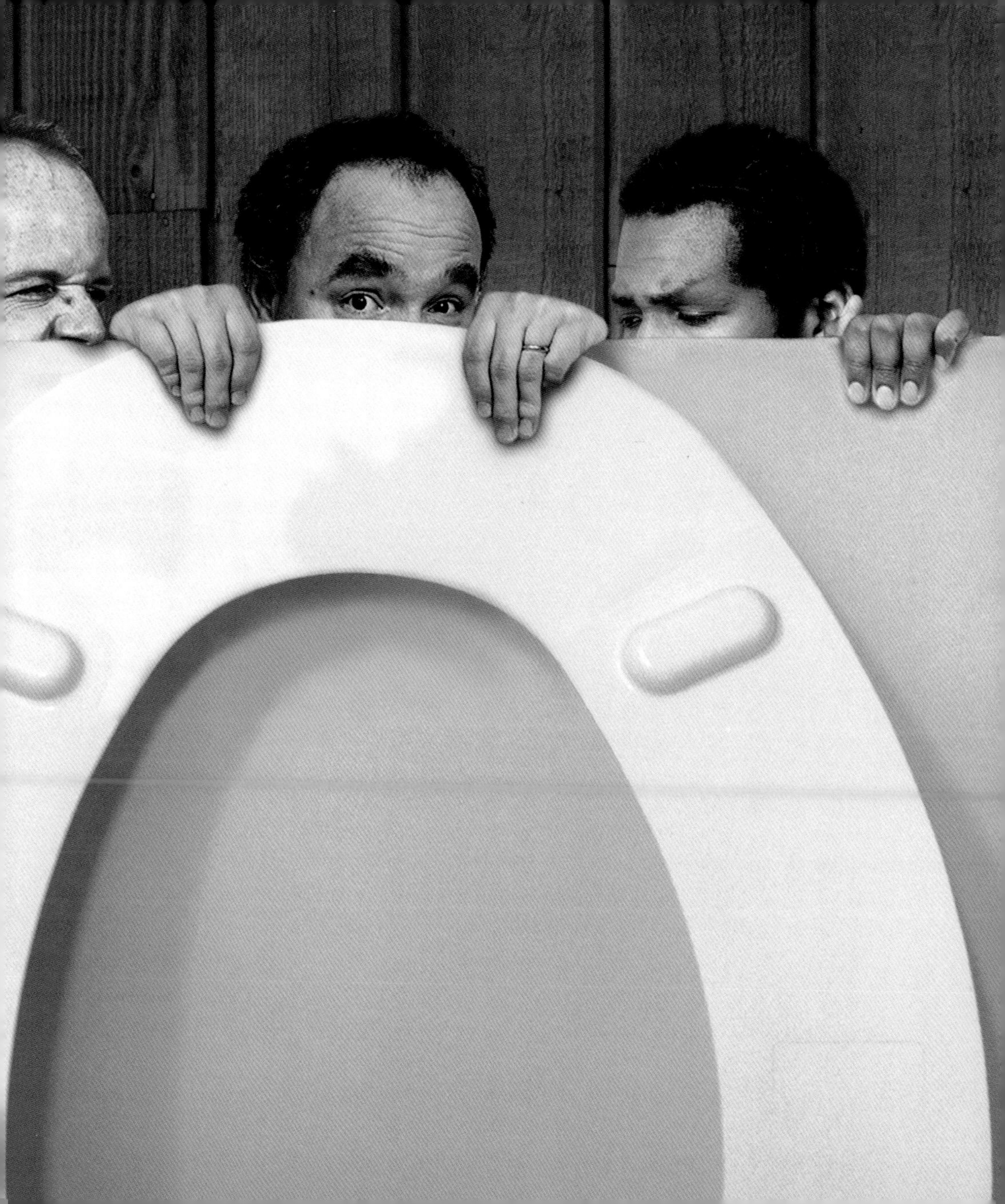

If

you

don't

know

where

the

BOYS

are *L o o k   f o r   t h e m   w h e r e*

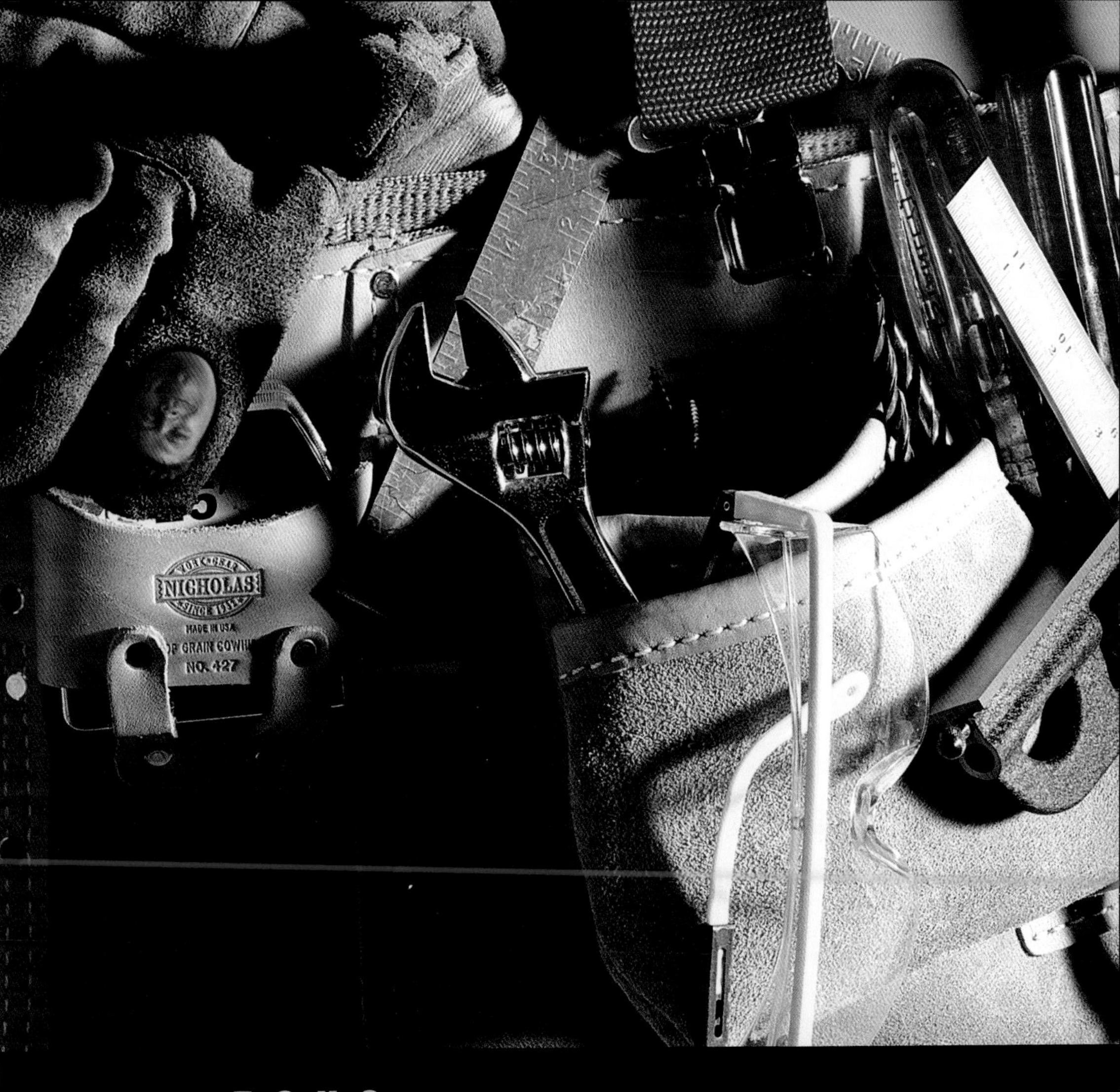

their **TOYS** *are.*

EVEN THE LITTLEST ONES *REQUIRE A LOT*

F VROOM.

The more important the gathering, the more likely he

12
5
9
8
3
2
11
1
ill be at the center.

You can hear little men

from Miami to Nome:

"I'm taking my ball

and going home."

17

The **WEEKDAY** *Persona*

The **WEEKEND** *Metamorphosis*

BASS
Finish Fast,
Martin a BGN Maestro
INSIDE
A final shot
PrepsPlus
PURPLE
Party
Lineu
SPRING TRAINING WORKOUTS
JAYHAWK
NOW FOR
Meek
FULL CIRCLE
MIZZOU SPORTS
SPORTS DAILY
Angry Umpires

Ten little pinheads

Standing in a row

Nine fall down;

One left to go.

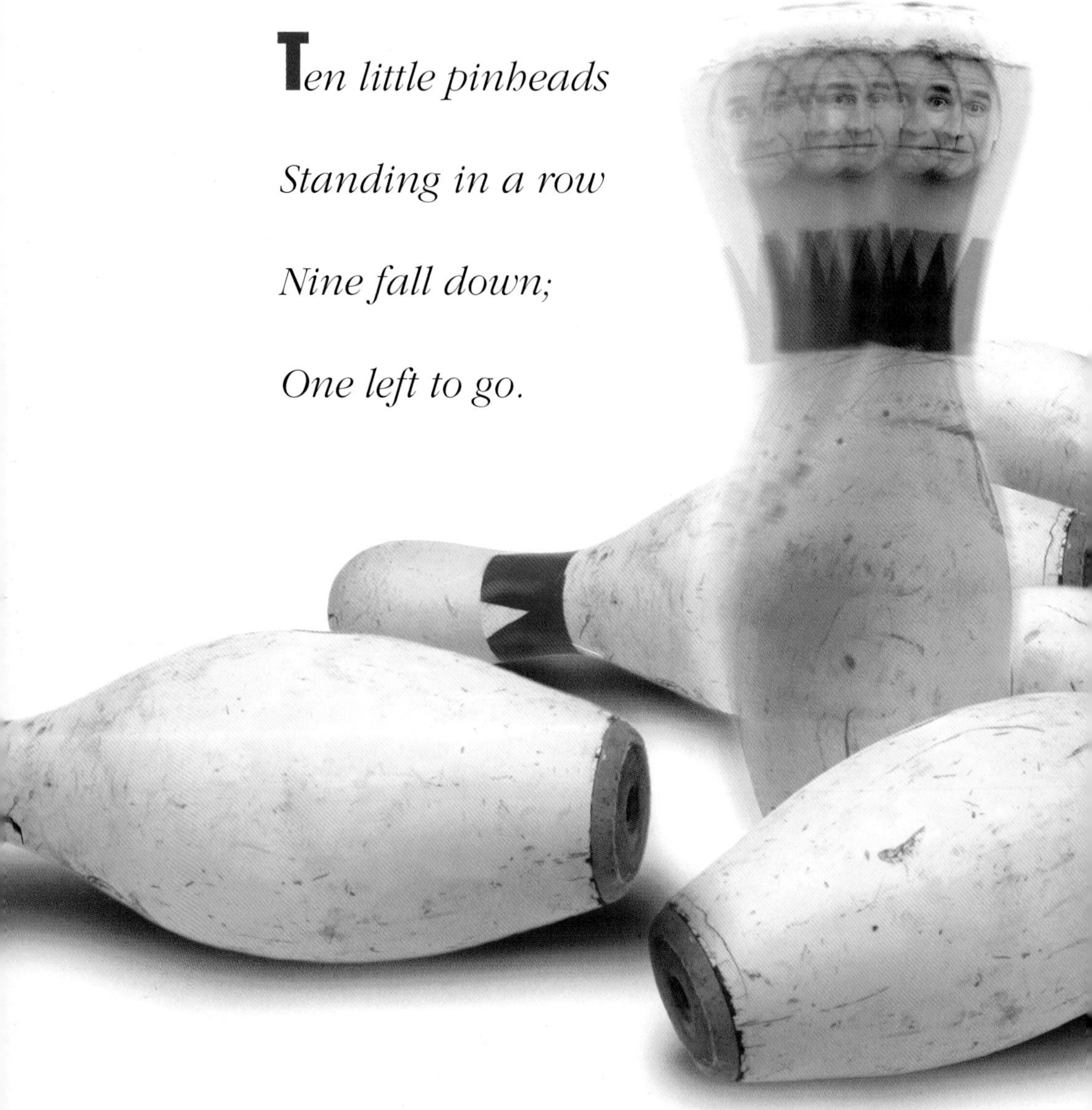

How'd nine pinheads

Take such a fall?

Seventeen Bud Lights

Before last call.

THERE MUST BE A WAY TO GET BABES WITHOUT GETTING A JOB...BABES AND A MERCEDES...NO, A

Naturally,

...A PORSCHE AND A MERCEDES...AND NINTENDO...NINTENDO 64, OF CO

he also has his higher dreams and aspirations...

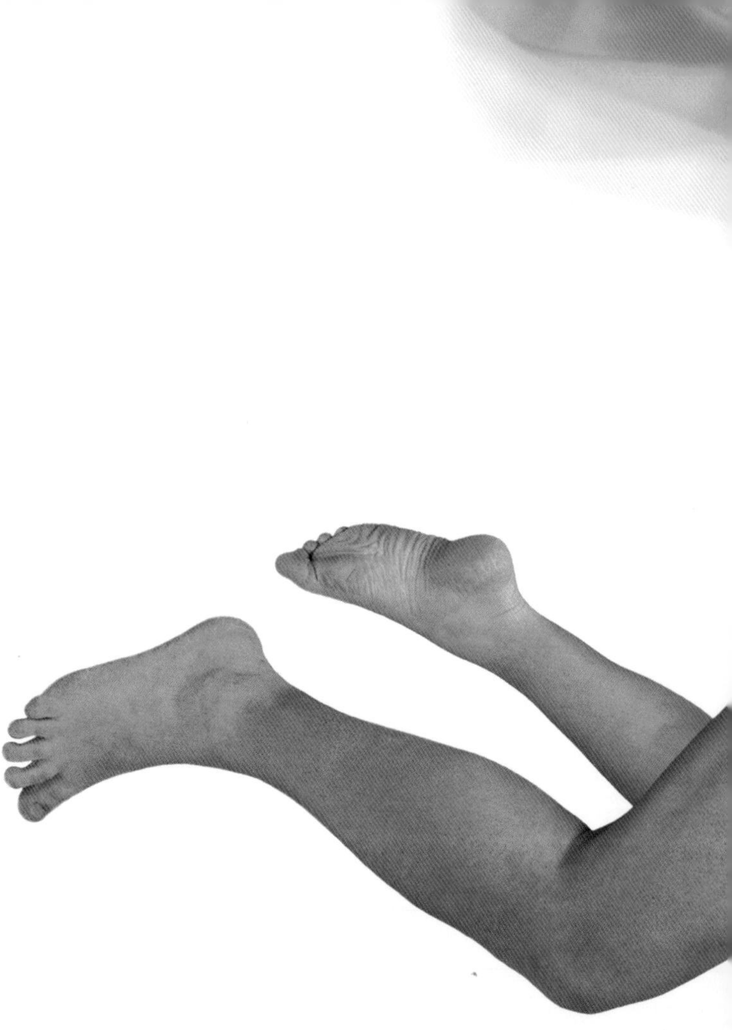

In certain private moments, he lets those

PECIAL *fantasies take wing.*

12
12

When it comes

to the manly sports,

HE IS FEARLESS:

he'll watch anything.

In his philosophy...

less is **DEFIN**

ELY NOT *more*

WHEAT
BEER
BOULEVARD
IA REFUND 5¢
Brewed
with the trad-
itional ingredients:
water, locally grown wheat,
two row barley malt, hops and yeast.

And **BIGGE**

s always **BETTER.**

There was a little male

Who was hearty and hale

Successes were his for

the trying.

And when he was well

The world was just swell

But when he was sick

He was

D Y I N G

Mother's
CONDENSED SOUP
HOMEMADE
CHICKEN SOUP
SERVING
SUGGESTION

Two **ALL B**

F *Fatties*

Whatever it was, he didn't mean it. Or he didn't mean it *that* way. Or he *did* mean it that way, but he didn't mean for you to hear it. Well, that is, not that there's anything you shouldn't *hear*, it's just that he didn't mean it. Whatever it was.

WINNING *isn't the* main thing.

GLOATING *is the* main thing.

They all have a favorite place. Funny that s

many of them have the *same* favorite place...

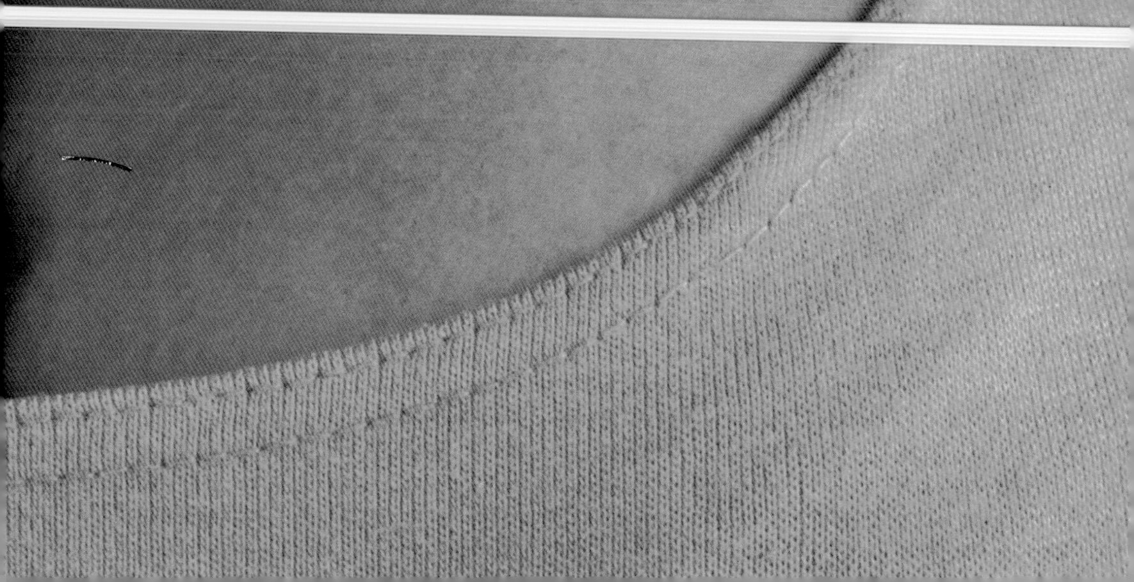

He dreams of attaining what he value

most...

E*nergy*

S*trength*

P*ower*

N*erves of Steel*

Baby don't **KNOW**

Where anything goes

So **HOW** can he

Put things away?

Wherever **THESE** are

When he's finished

With **THOSE**

Is exactly where

ALL THIS will stay.